THE
SEAWEED
COOKBOOK

A FIREFLY BOOK

Published by Firefly Books Ltd. 2019

First printing

Publisher Cataloging-in-Publication Data (U.S.)

Library of Congress Control Number: 2018951287

Library and Archives Canada Cataloguing in Publication

Pisani, Nicole, author
      The seaweed cookbook : discover the health benefits and uses
of seaweed, with 50 delicious recipes / Nicole Pisani & Kate Adams.
Includes index.
ISBN 978-0-2281-0091-1 (hardcover)
      1. Cooking (Marine algae). 2. Marine algae as food. 3. Marine
algae--Therapeutic use. 4. Cookbooks. I. Adams, Kate (Health
publisher), author II. Title.
TX402.P57 2019   641.6'98   C2018-904177-3

Published in the United States by
Firefly Books (U.S.) Inc.
P.O. Box 1338, Ellicott Station
Buffalo, New York 14205

Printed in China

Published in Canada by
Firefly Books Ltd.
50 Staples Avenue, Unit 1
Richmond Hill, Ontario L4B 0A7

First published in Great Britain by Aster, a division
of Octopus Publishing Group Ltd, Carmelite
House, 50 Victoria Embankment, London
EC4Y 0DZ

Consultant Publisher Kate Adams; Recipe
Developer and Food Stylist Nicole Pisani,
Food for Happiness; Additional Recipes Mariko
Bangerter and Oliver Pagani; Senior Designer
Jaz Bahra; Assistant Editor Nell Warner; Copy
Editor Clare Sayer; Photographer Issy Croker;
Food and Props Stylist Emily Ezekiel; Production
Manager Caroline Alberti

Picture credits: 7 from The Sea-Shore by William
S Furneaux, Longmans, Green & Co, London 1911;
9 Ralukatudor/ Dreamstime.com; 10 Jonathan
Austin Daniels/iStock; 14-15 raung/iStock

THE SEAWEED COOKBOOK

Discover the health benefits and uses of
seaweed, with 50 delicious recipes

**NICOLE PISANI
& KATE ADAMS**

FIREFLY BOOKS

CONTENTS

INTRODUCTION

Seaweed, or sea vegetables, are a wonderful wild food that have been foraged and cultivated by coastal peoples for as long as people have lived by the sea. Over millennia, the uses of seaweed have included being eaten as a nutritious food, as medicines and as fertilizer for other crops to grow more abundantly.

In Japan — the country we tend to think of first when it comes to eating seaweed — seaweed was such an integral part of life in 703 AD that people were able to pay their taxes in kelp. But it isn't just Asia where seaweed has long been a part of life. For example, in Mesoamerica, a mixture of seaweed and other medicinal herbs from a staggering 12,500 years ago was discovered by archeologists.

In Scotland, it is thought that seaweed was used as feed for sheep as far back as the Neolithic period, which was about 5,000 years ago. Seaweed was once such an important part of the Scottish rural economy that ale or porridge was poured into the sea to ensure a good harvest. Seaweed was used to help crops grow, to make soap and glass, and was eaten both raw and cooked.

> O God of the Sea,
> Put weed in the drawing wave
> To enrich the ground,
> To shower us with food.
> —Traditional religious Scottish chant

EDIBLE SEAWEEDS

There are well over 100 types of edible seaweed, from kombu to arame, Irish moss, laver, nori, dulse, wakami, sea lettuce and kelp.

In Japan, Korea and China, seaweed is considered part of the daily diet, while in Western countries it has fallen off most menus. However, the interest in seaweed both for flavor and nutrition, means that seaweed is beginning to make a comeback and consumption is on the rise throughout the world.

In Iceland, sheep graze on moss and seaweed; often the meat is then marinated in seaweed before cooking. In Wales, laverbread, made by mixing laverweed (a type of seaweed) with oats, is still very much a delicacy, and in Scotland, dulse has been used as a tonic for centuries and is now an increasingly popular seasoning; it is also being used in the artisan drinks industry as an ingredient for gin.

BELOW (CLOCKWISE FROM TOP LEFT): *Fucus nodosus, Codium tomentosum, Porphyra laciniata, Padina pavonia* and *Nitophyllum laceratum.*

In Ireland, Irish moss or carrageen is used for making gelatin and desserts. It is also used to make a drink for when you are under the weather. Irish moss drinks are also popular in the Caribbean, where it is combined with vanilla and nutmeg to make a restorative drink.

Seaweed is also gaining in popularity on the North American coasts, and in recent years, seaweed has even been the inspiration for the development of edible, i.e. non-plastic, water pods.

SEAWEED FARMING

Mentions of the cultivation of seaweed in Korea can be found in 15th century books, and in Japan — where the majority of seaweed farms exist today — it is thought that seaweed farming began in the mid-late 17th century in Tokyo Bay. Bamboo branches were thrown into the water to collect seaweed spores. After a few weeks these branches would then be moved to the river, where the seaweed would grow, aided by the nutrients in the river. Now that the demand for seaweed is rising, the sustainable cultivation of seaweed is growing in interest in

Europe and North America in particular. As with all the foods we consume, it is important to be aware of the source of seaweed. The quality of the seawater in which the seaweed is grown and harvested is significant because seaweed absorbs the nutrients of its environment.

THE HEALTH BENEFITS OF SEAWEED

In Chinese medicine, seaweed has been considered to have certain health properties for thousands of years, and has been used in folk medicines over many centuries.

ANCIENT WISDOM

Interestingly, seaweed is mentioned in both Chinese medicine and Scottish folk medicine as being beneficial for urinary infections, wet coughs and sore throats. In Scotland, an old remedy that was used for wet coughs was to soak carrageen (Irish moss) in warm milk and honey. Green laver, similar to nori, was used as a remedy for constipation, while bladderwrack would be held under hot running water into a bath until the little pockets dissolved to create a remedy for easing the pain of arthritis. Similarly, it would be soaked in a foot bath to soothe tired feet. In Ireland and the Caribbean, Irish moss is also a traditional ingredient for a tonic or pick-me-up, rather like chicken soup in many cultures.

MODERN TIMES

From a nutritional point of view, seaweeds are packed with vitamins and minerals. They are high in protein (particularly the red varieties), soluble fibre and essential fatty acids, while being low in calories.

Antioxidants

Seaweeds contain a variety of antioxidants, including vitamins C and E and a number of phytochemicals. Antioxidants absorb the free radicals that we are exposed to from pollution and toxins in our environment, causing cell and tissue damage and often leading to diseases such as cancer.

Minerals

Seaweeds are a good plant source of calcium, magnesium, potassium, copper and iron.

OPPOSITE: Nori is the Japanese name for edible seaweed species of the red alga genus *Porphyra*.

Prebiotic

In recent years, studies have begun to indicate that seaweeds may have prebiotic properties, helping to create a healthy environment of beneficial bacteria in the gut.

Chlorophyll

Chlorophyll-rich foods are a natural protection against radiation.

Alginate

Alginate, found in the brown varieties of seaweed, has been linked to strengthening gut mucus, which is good for maintaining the health of the gut wall. It also slows down digestion so that energy is released over time rather than in a short burst, making you feel fuller for longer.

Enzymes

The enzymes found in kombu, a type of kelp, help to pre-digest legumes during the cooking process, which reduces unwanted side effects such as gas and indigestion.

Iodine

Bladderwrack and other brown seaweeds are high in iodine, which is considered beneficial if you have a thyroid condition as it may help to boost metabolism. If you do have a thyroid condition or other health concerns, then it is advised to consult a medical practitioner before including seaweeds in your diet.

OPPOSITE: Kombu, or edible kelp, used in Japanese cuisine.

HOW TO COOK WITH SEAWEED

Seaweeds come in many different shapes, textures and flavors. There are a myriad of edible seaweed varieties now available in Asian markets, delis, health-food stores and online. You can even buy seaweed seasoning and oils. Here's a useful starter guide to some of the more popular varieties and how to cook with them.

Arame — this has a slightly sweet taste. Soak arame until soft and then slice and add to salads, vegetables or noodles.

Bladderwrack — this is a brown seaweed with "bladder" type pockets and quite a strong, salty and fishy taste. It is best steamed and goes well with fish. This type of seaweed is high in iodine, so you are not advised to consume it if you have a thyroid condition unless in consultation with a medical practitioner.

Dulse — grown mainly in northern Europe and North America, dulse is a versatile seaweed that can be used as a seasoning in flakes, pan-fried with oil as you would bacon or added to smoothies, soups and stews. It is also used in baking, where you can replace vanilla with dulse flakes soaked in dark rum. It can be pickled with other vegetables such as beets or radish, and makes a delicious salad dressing mixed with soy sauce and rice wine vinegar. If you come across fresh dulse it can be eaten raw in salads or as a side to fish and meat dishes. It turns from red to green when cooked.

Hijiki — it is advised to source certified organic *hijiki* because some types of this edible seaweed have been found to contain arsenic. It is a delicious seaweed with earthy qualities that mean it goes well with mushrooms, root vegetables and rice. The simplest way to cook hijiki is to soak it for 30 minutes in fresh water, rinse and then braise for 15 minutes with soy sauce, mirin and sake, along with some vegetables. This is called *hijiki no nimono*.

Irish moss or **carrageen** — a type of seaweed used as a thickener, especially in desserts.

Kelp — has a rich, savory umami flavor. Kombu is a member of the kelp family and is often the basis for the stock known as "dashi," which then becomes an ingredient for any dish that requires a vegetable stock. It is a delicious, clean-tasting broth. Kombu is also very useful for adding to beans and legumes during cooking as it helps to pre-digest them. Kelp powder is great for adding to smoothies and is a great seasoning alternative to salt.

Nori — another versatile, salty seaweed. In sheet form it can be toasted as a snack or rolled for sushi; it is also available as nori sprinkles and used as a seasoning for a hit of umami.

Sea lettuce — you may be able to find this fresh and ready to eat; otherwise it just needs soaking until al dente and added to salads or at the last moment to broths. If you find sea lettuce in sheet form, it is also a wonderful way to wrap fish for cooking whole.

Sea spaghetti or thongweed/buttonweed — this is a type of seaweed that has the appearance of a dark-colored spaghetti and can be boiled along with regular spaghetti or steamed (for 25–30 minutes). It is excellent when stirred into pasta, mixed with lots of stir-fried vegetables or with a raw salad.

Wakame — this seaweed has a salty-sweet flavor and just needs soaking. It is very good for adding to rice dishes, or add a few strips to a stir-fry or stir into a fish stew before serving. Wakame is also excellent for pickling or making relishes.

NEXT PAGE: A seaweed farm in Nusa Penida, Bali.

BREAKFASTS

BROWN BUTTER GRANOLA

You could swap the brown butter for coconut oil in this recipe, but it does add a wonderful extra layer of caramelized flavor that goes really well with the subtle saltiness of the furikake, which is a mix of sesame seeds and nori. Groats are the hulled kernels of cereal grains and are similar to brown rice, maintaining a bite when cooked.

2¾ cups (250 g) jumbo rolled oats

½ cup (100 g) buckwheat groats

⅓ cup (50 g) ground almonds

½ cup (50 g) almonds, roughly chopped

2 tbsp Furikake (see page 33)

3½ tbsp (50 g) unsalted butter

2 tbsp maple syrup

Preheat the oven to 275°F (140°C) and line a large sheet pan with parchment paper.

Mix all the dry ingredients together in a large bowl.

Heat the butter in a small saucepan over low heat and when melted, allow it to gradually turn brown and nutty. Take it off the heat and stir in the maple syrup. Pour this mixture into the dry ingredients and stir thoroughly so that all the oats, buckwheat, nuts and furikake are evenly coated and sticking together in small clusters.

Evenly spread the granola in the lined sheet pan without breaking up the clusters. Bake for about 1 hour until golden and just crunchy. Leave to cool and then gently bring up the sides of the paper to transfer the granola to an airtight jar.

RHUBARB COMPOTE

According to flavor experts, seaweed goes with a number of different fruits, including cherries, apples and rhubarb. Perhaps it is the combination of sweet with umami savory that works together. This compote is delicious both with yogurt or granola for breakfast, or with ice cream for dessert.

---

4 large (500 g) rhubarb stalks, rinsed, trimmed and roughly chopped

3 tbsp honey

1 tsp dried dulse flakes

Add the rhubarb pieces to a saucepan while still wet. Place over a low heat, bring to a gentle simmer and cook for about 10 minutes, or until soft.

Stir in the honey and dulse flakes and continue to simmer for a few more minutes, stirring occasionally. Take it off the heat and cover with a lid to cool.

Store it in the refrigerator in an airtight container for up to a week.

SEAWEED MUFFINS

These savory muffins are full of the umami flavors of both seaweed flakes and sharp Cheddar cheese, along with a little heat from wasabi — a type of horseradish that, in paste form, is a more familiar accompaniment to sushi.

2 cups (250 g) wholegrain spelt flour

1 tbsp baking powder

1 tsp fine sea salt

1 tbsp nori sprinkle

1 tbsp dried dulse flakes, plus extra to serve

1 tsp wasabi or mustard powder

1 cup (100 g) Cheddar cheese, grated

1 egg

½ cup (100 ml) olive oil

¾ cup (250 g) plain yogurt

Preheat the oven to 400°F (200°C) and line a muffin pan with 8 paper muffin liners.

Put the flour, baking powder, salt, nori, dulse, wasabi and grated Cheddar in a large bowl and mix well. Mix the egg, oil and yogurt together in another bowl, and then add this to the flour mixture and combine thoroughly.

Divide the mixture between the liners in the muffin pan. Bake in the oven for about 25 minutes until golden and just firm to the touch. Remove from the pan and cool on a wire rack before serving garnished with extra dulse flakes on top.

———

MISO OATS
WITH SEAWEED KIMCHI

In Asia, breakfast is traditionally a savory affair, such as the miso porridge at the base of this recipe. Adding shredded seaweed to kimchi adds extra umami flavor, texture and health.

For the seaweed kimchi

1 Napa cabbage

1 tbsp Seaweed Salt (see page 32)

0.35 oz (10 g) dried wakame

5 tbsp (25 g) Korean red pepper powder

3 tbsp (50 g) Korean anchovy sauce

3½ tbsp (50 ml) water

1 tbsp grated fresh ginger

1 carrot, grated

First sterilize a jar for the kimchi: place a clean jar and its lid upright in the sink and pour over just-boiled water from the kettle. Leave to air dry.

Slice the cabbage into ½ inch (1 cm) rounds. Toss with the Seaweed Salt, making sure it is evenly covered, and leave at room temperature for about 6 hours.

Rinse the salt off the cabbage and drain well. Soak the wakame in water for 10 minutes, then drain and slice thinly. Mix the Korean red pepper powder, anchovy sauce and water together to make a runny paste. Add the garlic and ginger, then pour this mixture over the cabbage, grated carrot and wakame. Mix together thoroughly.

Transfer to your sterilized jar, leaving about 1 inch (2.5 cm) gap at the top. Press down on the cabbage so that the liquid just covers the vegetables. Seal and leave to sit for a day at room temperature. You can then store in the refrigerator for up to a month — it is ready to eat after the first day.

For the miso oats

2 tsp peanut oil

1 shallot, chopped

⅓ cup (55 g) oat groats, soaked overnight, rinsed and drained

1 tsp white or brown miso paste

1¼ cups (300 ml) just-boiled water

1 egg

Seaweed Salt (see page 32), to serve

For the miso oats, heat half the peanut oil in a saucepan and gently fry the shallot for 5 minutes, before stirring in the oat groats. Add the miso paste and stir, then add the just-boiled water. Bring to a boil, then lower the heat to simmer for about 20 minutes, or until the oat groats are tender.

Heat the remaining oil in a nonstick frying pan and, once hot, fry the egg for 2–3 minutes until the white is cooked.

Serve the miso oats in a bowl, topped with a spoonful of seaweed kimchi, the fried egg and a little Seaweed Salt to taste.

_____

TAMAGOYAKI

This might sound like a rather complicated omelette, and the rolling does take a little bit of practice, but it's a really delicious way of serving eggs. If you did prefer the option of an easier omelette, then a great seaweed to use is wakame, soaked to soften, cut into small strips and added to the center of the omelette before folding over.

6 eggs
1 tbsp mirin
1 tbsp brown sugar
vegetable oil, for frying
2 sheets of nori

For the dipping sauce
1 tsp brown sugar
1 tbsp + 1 tsp (20 ml) tamari
1 teaspoon sesame seeds
1 teaspoon poppy seeds

In a bowl, beat the eggs with the mirin and sugar.

Pour vegetable oil into a nonstick frying pan, place over high heat and swirl until the base of the pan is evenly coated. When the pan is really hot, pour about a third of the egg mixture into the pan and spread it evenly by tilting the pan in a circular motion. Leave it for 1–2 minutes until the bottom is cooked but the center is still runny.

Add a sheet of nori seaweed to the center. Roll up the egg starting from one edge. After rolling a few times, move the roll to the right side of the pan. Carefully lift up the remainder of the seaweed that has not been rolled yet and pour more egg mixture on to the empty side of the pan so that it overlaps with the cooked side of the egg. Allow to cook for a couple of minutes until set and then add another sheet of nori. Continue to roll and move to the side until all the mixture is used up.

Place the rolled egg on a flat bamboo mat and roll the mat over and around to shape the roll. (If you don't have a bamboo mat, you can skip this step.) Leave it to cool for at least 10 minutes before slicing. Meanwhile, make the dipping sauce by dissolving the brown sugar in the tamari, add the seeds and serve alongside the tamagoyaki.

LAVER BUBBLE AND SQUEAK

Laverbread is a traditional Welsh recipe made with oats and the
seaweed found in abundance on the Welsh coast, similar to nori but
darker. Bubble and squeak is a traditional British recipe for using up
leftover roasted vegetables and cabbage or Brussels sprouts. That might
not sound like a breakfast dish but these patties are amazing for brunch
when topped with an egg and served with lots of fresh baby spinach

1 small (50 g) sweet potato,
scrubbed

1 small onion, sliced

1 tbsp dried laver or nori sprinkle

½ tsp sea salt

3 tbsp olive oil

½ cup (80 g) pancetta, cubed
(optional)

1 cup (100 g) Savoy cabbage or
spring greens, shredded

generous ⅓ cup (50 g) oatmeal

1 tbsp (20 g) unsalted butter, plus
extra if needed

2 eggs

3 cup (100 g) baby spinach

2 tbsp hollandaise, to serve

sea salt (optional)

Preheat the oven to 425°F (220°C).

Roughly chop the sweet potatoes and toss with the
sliced onion, seaweed flakes, sea salt and 1 tablespoon
of the olive oil. Spread out in a roasting pan and roast
for 35–45 minutes, or until golden at the edges. Set aside
until cool enough to handle (leave the oven on).

Meanwhile, heat a little olive oil in a frying pan, add the
pancetta and cook over medium heat until browned,
then add the cabbage and sauté for about 5 minutes until
just tender. Put the oatmeal into a shallow bowl.

In a large bowl, mash the sweet potatoes to a coarse
consistency. Mix in the onions, pancetta and cabbage.
Shape this mixture into 2 or 4 patties, depending on
whether you prefer them small or large, and then press
each patty into the oatmeal so that all sides are covered.

Melt the butter and another tablespoon of the oil in an
ovenproof frying pan over medium heat. When hot,
carefully place the patties in the pan and cook for about
7 minutes on each side until golden. To make sure the
patties are warm all the way through, transfer them to
a sheet pan and place on the top shelf of the oven for
another 5 minutes.

For the hollandaise sauce (optional)

3 egg yolks

2 tbsp of any white vinegar of your choice

½ tsp cracked black pepper

2 tbsp (100 g) melted butter

To make your own hollandaise sauce, whisk the yolks, vinegar and pepper in a bowl placed over a saucepan of simmering water (it should not touch the water) until it has a pale ribbon-like consistency. Drizzle the melted butter very slowly into the egg yolks, whisking constantly until thick and smooth. Set aside for later.

Poach or fry the eggs as you prefer and either shred the spinach or wilt with a little butter and salt in a hot pan. Divide the spinach between two plates, add the patties and serve with an egg on top and some hollandaise sauce.

VALENCIA SEAWEED EGGS

Here is a super-quick and tasty way to use a little seaweed in combination with chili and garlic for a very healthy omelette. Use more or less seaweed as you get to know your taste for this healthy ingredient.

1 tbsp dried wakame flakes (or any type of seaweed flake)

4 large eggs

2 tbsp olive oil, plus extra for drizzling

1 garlic clove, thinly sliced

½ red chili, finely chopped (or more, to taste)

sea salt and freshly ground black pepper

Soak the seaweed in a bowl of water for 5 minutes, or until softened. Drain and pat dry with paper towels.

Crack the eggs into a bowl and lightly beat with a fork. Season with a pinch of salt and pepper.

Place a large frying pan over medium heat and add the olive oil. Add the garlic and chili and fry for a minute until fragrant. Add the soaked seaweed and stir for 20 seconds so the seaweed takes on the flavors of the garlic and chili.

Add all of the egg mixture to the pan and make an omelette by pulling in the edges with a spatula to allow the runny egg to cover the base of the pan. When the surface of the omelette is almost fully cooked, fold it in half and slide it out of the pan.

Drizzle a little more olive oil on top and serve.

FURIKAKE OATCAKES

These oatcakes are delicious with soft cheeses. Homemade oatcakes tend to be a little more crumbly so when you transfer to a wire rack for cooling, using a spatula or similarly flat-bottomed utensil is a good idea.

1 cup (100 g) medium rolled oats
½ cup (50 g) oat flour
3½ tbsp (50 g) Furikake
(see page 33)
¼ cup (50 ml) extra virgin olive oil
all-purpose flour, for dusting

Preheat the oven to 350°F (180°C) and line two sheet pans with parchment paper.

Mix all the dry ingredients together in a large bowl. Make a well in the middle and pour in the olive oil. Add enough water, a little at a time, to bring the mixture together to just form a dough.

Turn the dough out onto a lightly floured surface and knead gently before dusting with flour and rolling out to a thickness of about ¼ inch (5 mm).

Cut out rounds with a cookie cutter and arrange on the lined sheet pans. Bake for 30 minutes, turning the trays halfway through, until golden. Remove from the oven and cool for a couple of minutes before transferring to a wire rack to cool fully.

CONDIMENTS & SNACKS

MAKES 3½ CUPS (100 G)

———

SEAWEED SALT

Seaweed salt is a fantastic seasoning to have on hand for finishing any dish, from fish to steak to scrambled eggs. Seaweed is still salty but contains lots of other nutrients, too, so it's a great combination.

2¾ tbsp (50 g) sea salt flakes
3¼ cups (50 g) dried dulse flakes or nori sprinkle

Mix the sea salt and seaweed together and store in an airtight container. Use within 2 years.

MAKES ABOUT 1 CUP (170 G)

———

GOMASHIO

Another type of Japanese seasoning, gomashio is a combination of seaweed, salt and sesame. This is perfect for stir-fries, egg dishes, tofu and even pasta.

5½ tbsp (50 g) white sesame seeds
½ tbsp (10 g) sea salt flakes
2 tsp kelp powder

Toast the sesame seeds in a hot dry frying pan until they turn golden and just begin to pop. Grind in a pestle and mortar along with the sea salt and kelp powder. Transfer to an airtight jar and keep for up to a year; shake to combine before using.

FURIKAKE

This Japanese seasoning combines sesame seeds and seaweed, with
a little shiso added for extra umami. You can sprinkle this on almost
anything for added crunch and flavor, from a simple salad of greens
to steamed rice, sautéed kale, miso soup or over tofu cubes.

2¼ tbsp (20 g) black sesame
seeds

2¼ tbsp (20 g) white sesame
seeds

3¼ cups (50 g) nori sprinkle

1 tsp (5 g) shiso condiment

Mix all the ingredients together and store in an airtight
container for up to 6 months.

SEAWEED OIL

This is such a simple recipe, but it's a great way to instantly add the
flavor of seaweed to dressings or stir-fries. It's also excellent when
used to pan-fry fish.

2 cups (500 ml) extra virgin olive
oil (or your oil of choice)

1 oz (30 g) dried kombu

2 tbsp nori sprinkle

Decant the oil into a clip-top rubber sealed jar. Add the
kombu and nori sprinkle and leave to infuse for at least
2 weeks. You can then strain into an oil bottle or simply
leave the seaweed in the oil to infuse further.

SEAWEED RELISH

This recipe is inspired by Gentlemen's Relish, which is basically an anchovy butter that is great to have on hand to add an instant hit of amazing flavor, for example at the end of cooking a steak. This version is also delicious on toast with an aperitif.

---

4 tbsp (50 g) butter

2 tbsp mixed dried seaweed flakes

4–6 (25 g) anchovy fillets, finely chopped

pinch of cayenne pepper

pinch of ground cinnamon

pinch of grated nutmeg

pinch of ground ginger

1½ tbsp (25 g) tamari

toasted sourdough, to serve

Melt the butter in a small saucepan over a low heat and then mix in all the other ingredients. Pour into a shallow butter dish and refrigerate.

To serve, remove the relish from the refrigerator and bring up to room temperature. Toast slices of sourdough and spread with the seaweed butter.

SEAWEED SKYR DIP

In Iceland, skyr is a fermented and strained yogurt that is high in protein and extremely low in fat and is used in many dishes. Seaweed is also an ingredient local to Iceland and thought to be one of the reasons why Icelandic lamb is so tasty, as sheep in Iceland eat seaweed as part of their diet. We have combined these two very Icelandic ingredients to make a simple dip for raw vegetables or crackers.

generous ¾ cup (200 g) skyr yogurt (or plain yogurt)

1 tbsp nori sprinkle

juice of ½ lemon

½ cucumber, diced

small handful of mint leaves, finely chopped

sea salt and black pepper

raw vegetable sticks or crackers, to serve

Mix all the dip ingredients together, then taste and adjust the seasoning, if needed.

Chill until needed (it will keep in the refrigerator for up to 3 days) and serve with a selection of fresh vegetables or crackers.

MAKES ABOUT 2 CUPS (300 G)

————

PICKLED SEAWEED

Having pickled seaweed on hand is so useful: add it to any
Asian rice or noodle dish, enjoy with cheese and crackers or
add to miso or dashi-based soups.

1.5 oz (30 g) dried kombu
¾ cup + 1½ tbsp (200 ml) water
⅔ cup (150 ml) brown rice vinegar
½ cup (100 g) brown sugar
1 tsp sea salt
¼ tsp shichimi togarashi
 (Japanese seven-spice
 powder)*
1 tsp (5 g) dried dulse
2 red chilies
2 shallots, sliced
½ cucumber, sliced

To sterilize your pickling jar, place a clean jar in the sink
and pour over just-boiled water from the kettle. Leave
to air dry.

Soak the kombu in the water for 3 hours. Drain, reserving
the liquid, slice into strips and set aside.

Bring the dashi (the liquid that the kombu was soaking
in) to a boil, lower to a simmer and add the vinegar, sugar,
salt and shichimi togarashi. Once the sugar has dissolved,
take off the heat.

Meanwhile, place the kombu, dulse, chillies, shallots and
cucumber in the dry sterilized pickling jar.

Pour the pickling liquid over the kombu, leave to cool for
20 minutes then close the lid. Store in the refrigerator for
up to a month.

*Japanese seven-spice powder, shichimi
togarashi, is different than Chinese
five-spice and Lebanese seven-spice.
The versatile Japanese seven-spice
blends chili pepper, dried orange peel,
black sesame seeds, white sesame seeds,
Japanese pepper (sansho), ginger, and
seaweed. It can be found at Japanese
food shops but be sure to buy shichimi
togarashi, not ichimi togarashi, which is
plain chili powder.

SEAWEED AIOLI

Aioli is mayonnaise flavored with garlic. You can add other flavors such as basil or, as in this recipe, a hint of seaweed. It's delicious with fish fingers or in egg sandwiches.

1 garlic clove
¼ tsp sea salt
1 egg yolk
1 tsp Dijon mustard
1 cup (250 ml) extra virgin olive oil
1 cup (250 ml) olive oil
juice of ½ a lemon
1 tbsp mixed dried seaweed flakes

Crush the garlic clove with the sea salt in a pestle and mortar to form a paste.

Whisk the egg yolk with the mustard in a bowl. Gradually add the oil, starting with just a drop at a time and whisking continuously. When you have added about half the oils, squeeze in the lemon juice and then continue to add the remaining oil in a thin stream, whisking all the time.

When you have added all the oil, mix in the garlic paste and seaweed flakes.

Store in an airtight jar in the refrigerator for up to a week.

SEAWEED TARTAR SAUCE

Tartar sauce is traditionally made with mayonnaise and pickles. We used olive oil instead of mayonnaise and it works very well, delicious with any fish or with cold meat and cheese.

scant 1 cup (75 g) fresh dulse or soaked wakame, finely chopped

2–3 (50 g) baby dill pickles, finely chopped

3 tbsp (25 g) capers, finely chopped

2 garlic cloves, finely chopped

1 shallot, finely chopped

2¾ tbsp (40 ml) apple cider vinegar

4 tbsp (60 ml) extra virgin olive oil

1 tbsp brown sugar

sea salt, to taste

Simply combine all the ingredients in a bowl, adjusting to your own taste.

If you prefer a finely chopped consistency, pulse the seaweed, pickles, capers, garlic and shallot in a food processor before adding the vinegar, oil and brown sugar.

SOUPS

SEAWEED BROTH
WITH NORI TOAST

This broth is a delicious starter to any meal, or when you just
feel like a very light lunch or supper. You can add some noodles,
rice or tofu if you want a little more substance.

For the dashi broth

3 inch (8 cm) piece of kombu

1¾ cup (400 ml) water

¾ cup (10 g) dried bonito flakes
(optional)

1 tbsp dried wakame, soaked in
water for 10 minutes

2 tsp white miso

1 spring onion, thinly sliced

1 cup (40 g) baby salad leaves, to
serve

For the nori toast

½ tbsp sesame oil

½ tbsp tamari

2 sushi nori sheets

4 tsp Furikake (see page 33)

2 tsp dried chili flakes

Combine the kombu and water in a saucepan. Leave it
to sit for about 25–30 minutes, until the kombu softens,
then bring to a simmer over medium heat. Remove from
the heat and discard the kombu. Add the bonito flakes, if
using, and stir once to submerge them. Bring to a gentle
boil, reduce the heat and simmer about 5 minutes. Remove from the heat and set aside.

Strain the dashi (your broth) through a strainer into a
bowl. Clean the saucepan and then return the dashi to
the pan. Drain the wakame and add it to the pan, bring
to a simmer and then remove from the heat. Submerge a
strainer in the broth, add the miso to the strainer and stir
to liquify the miso then press through the strainer until
the miso is dissolved into the broth.

Divide the soup among bowls and garnish with spring
onions and baby leaves.

For the nori toasts, preheat the oven to 275°F (140°C).
Whisk the oil and tamari together and brush the shiny
sides of the nori sheets. Sprinkle the Furikake and chili
flakes over the same side of the sheets. Place the sheets
shiny side up directly on the middle shelf of the oven and
bake for 15 minutes. Remove from the oven and leave to
cool before enjoying.

MISO MUSHROOM

The umami flavor of miso and dulse is the perfect complement to earthy cremini mushrooms. Being a fermented food, miso has the added benefit of nourishing your gut flora.

½ cup (50 g) fresh shiitake or wild mushrooms

1½ tbsp (20 g) unsalted butter

scant 2½ cups (200 g) cremini mushrooms

1 tsp balsamic vinegar

1¼ cups (300 ml) hot vegetable stock

1 tbsp dried laver or dulse flakes, plus extra to serve

½ tbsp (10 g) white miso paste

scant ¾ cup (160 ml) almond milk

If using equivalent dried shiitake or wild mushrooms, soak them in hot water for a few minutes then drain, reserving the soaking liquid.

Melt the butter in a saucepan over a medium-low heat. Add all the mushrooms and cook for 10 minutes — this allows them to caramelize a little.

Deglaze the pan with the balsamic vinegar, remove about a quarter of the cooked mushrooms and set aside. Add the hot stock, reserved mushroom soaking liquid (if using), laver or dulse flakes and miso paste to the pan. Continue to cook for another 5 minutes.

Remove from the heat and leave to rest for 10 minutes (this allows the flavors to come together). Add the almond milk and blend with an immersion blender. If you like a really smooth consistency, pass through a strainer.

Reheat the soup to serve. Reheat the set aside mushrooms and divide the soup and mushrooms between bowls. Garnish with a few dried laver or dulse flakes to serve.

SPICY GALBI TANG
WITH SEAWEED

Galbi tang is a traditional Korean soup made with beef. The delicious, delicately spiced broth you end up with at the end is worth the effort.

3⅓ lbs (1.5 kg) beef short ribs

12 cups (2.75 l) water

2 cooking onions, halved

4 garlic cloves, halved

thumb-sized piece of fresh ginger, thinly sliced

3 cups (1 small) daikon, chopped into medium chunks

12 cups (2.75 l) water

6 spring onions, chopped

0.25 oz (5 g) dried wakame

2 tbsp Korean hot pepper flakes (or more, to taste)

1 tbsp white sesame seeds

freshly ground black pepper

3 spring onions, thinly sliced, to serve

Bring a large saucepan of water (enough to cover the ribs) to a boil. Once boiling, add the ribs and blanch them for 10 minutes. Strain the ribs, reserving the water in a large jug or similar, and wash each rib to remove any excess fat. Clean the pan as well.

Put the ribs back into the clean pan with the onions, garlic, ginger and radish and pour over the reserved water, making sure everything is covered. Bring to a boil and cook over a medium-high heat for 1 hour.

After an hour, strain the broth through a fine-meshed strainer into a large bowl and skim off any remaining fat that floats to the surface. Discard the cooking onions and garlic but keep the radish and ginger and add these to the bowl. Remove the meat from the bones and return to the pan, along with the chopped spring onions. Pour over the broth, including the radish and ginger and then add the wakame, Korean pepper flakes and sesame seeds and season with black pepper. Place the pan back over a low heat.

The broth is ready when the wakame becomes hydrated in a few minutes. To serve, spoon the meat and the vegetables into individual bowls and top up with the broth. Finish by scattering with the sliced spring onions.

———

CHILLED APPLE SOUP
WITH SEAWEED TARTAR SAUCE

One of the fruit flavors that goes well with seaweed is apple, so we have adapted the more traditional "curried" apple soup, using a little Japanese seven-spice powder to add the heat and adding the seaweed in the garnishes.

1 tbsp olive oil

½ onion, sliced

2½ (600 g) Braeburn apples

½ tsp shichimi togarashi (Japanese seven-spice powder)

2 cups (500 ml) hot vegetable or chicken stock

pinch of Seaweed Salt (see page 32)

juice of ½ lemon

To serve

Seaweed Tartar sauce (see page 43)

Furikake (see page 33)

Heat the olive oil in a large saucepan, add the onion and cook gently for 10 minutes until soft but still translucent. Meanwhile, peel and core the apples.

Add the apples and shichimi togarashi to the onions and stir for a minute before adding the hot stock. Bring to a boil, then reduce the heat and simmer for about 30 minutes, or until the apples are very soft. Season with a good pinch of Seaweed Salt, leave to cool a little and puree with an immersion blender until smooth. If you like a very smooth soup, pass the blended soup through a strainer before allowing to cool fully.

Once cooled, add the lemon juice to taste. Chill before serving with a spoonful of Seaweed Tartar sauce and sprinkle of Furikake.

KOMBU DASHI
WITH SPIRULINA RICE AND SALMON

If you don't have spirulina powder on hand then this recipe works
very well without it — we loved the color it gave to the rice.

2 pieces of dried kombu

½ cup + 2 tbsp (150 ml) water

⅓ cup (60 g) brown rice

½ tsp spirulina powder (optional)

1 salmon fillet

Seaweed Salt (see page 32), or
    sea salt

1 tsp olive oil

1 tsp unsalted butter

1 tsp tamari

freshly ground black pepper

nasturtium leaves, to garnish
    (optional)

Combine the kombu and water in a saucepan. Leave to sit until the kombu softens, about 30 minutes. Bring to a boil, then take off the heat and remove and discard the kombu, reserving the broth.

Meanwhile, wash the brown rice a few times in cold water and then cook according to the packet instructions. Brown rice takes longer to cook than white rice and has a nutty bite to it. Put the hot rice into a large bowl and add the spirulina, if using, mixing thoroughly.

Season the salmon fillet with Seaweed Salt. Place a nonstick pan over a medium-high heat and add the olive oil. When it's really hot, place the salmon fillet skin-side down in the pan. Cook (don't move it around the pan) until you see the flesh of the salmon turn light pink half way up the fillet. Turn the fillet over and add the butter to the pan. If you like your salmon a little rare in the middle, take off the heat after about 30 seconds, longer if you prefer it cooked all the way through. Take off the heat and place it skin-side down on some paper towels to absorb any excess oil.

To serve, place the rice in the center of a bowl. Place the salmon on top and pour in the dashi broth. Add a splash of tamari and season with a little Seaweed Salt and black pepper. Garnish with nasturtium leaves, if using.

———

CHOWDER

"Chowder" comes from the French *chaudière*, meaning
"cauldron," or the pot the soup is made in. Breton fisherman
were known in North America for making a soup with their
catch of the day, and in this recipe the kombu infuses the flavor
of the sea into the poaching milk for the fish.

1 large (200 g) Russet potato, diced

1 tsp coconut oil

1 tsp unsalted butter

6 baby leeks

1¾ cups (400 ml) milk or coconut milk

0.1 oz (3 g) strip of kombu

7 oz (200 g) undyed smoked haddock

sea salt and black pepper

Furikake (*see* page 33), to serve

Bring a saucepan of salted water to a boil, add the potatoes and simmer until tender. Drain well and set aside.

Heat the coconut oil in a grill pan, and grill the baby leeks for about 5–7 minutes until charred.

Add the milk and kombu to a large pan along with the haddock, which should be just covered by the milk. Bring to a boil, then reduce the heat and simmer for 4 minutes until just cooked. Cover, remove from the heat and set aside to rest for a few minutes.

Remove the fish from the milk and gently flake it. Add half the flaked fish and half the potatoes to a food processor and blend with enough of the poaching milk to form a smooth soup consistency. Season to taste.

To serve, carefully combine the smooth soup base with the remaining potatoes and the baby leeks. Divide between bowls, top with the remaining flaked fish and season with the Furikake.

VEGETARIAN

PICKLED SEAWEED SALAD

This salad recipe was inspired by Pickled Seaweed (*see* page 41).
You can swap the seaweed "bacon" — a type of red algae that, when
cooked, has a distinctly bacon-like taste — for pancetta, if preferred.

2 large eggs

0.9 oz (25 g) seaweed "bacon" or
2.5 oz (75 g) pancetta, diced

1½ cups (100 g) pea shoots

3 cups (100 g) baby spinach

½ cup (80 g) Pickled Seaweed
(*see* page 41)

To serve

sea salt

dried seaweed flakes

extra virgin olive oil

To soft-boil the eggs, bring a saucepan of water to a boil,
add the eggs, and reduce to a rapid simmer. Cook for 7
minutes. If you prefer hard-boiled eggs, simmer for 9
minutes. Drain, cool under cold running water and then
peel and halve. Set aside.

Pan-fry the seaweed "bacon" (or pancetta) until crisp.

In a large mixing bowl, gently combine the seaweed
"bacon" with the pea shoots, baby spinach and Pickled
Seaweed. Arrange the salad in a shallow dish.

Place the halved eggs on the salad and serve scattered
with a little sea salt, some seaweed flakes and a drizzle
of extra virgin olive oil.

SAVORY BAKED CHEESECAKE

As seaweed goes with both eggs and cheese, this recipe is a delicious way to enjoy all three. It is a great sharing dish.

For the base

1½ tbsp (20 g) chilled unsalted butter, cut into ¾ inch (2 cm) dice, plus extra for greasing

3 digestive biscuits, roughly crumbled

¼ cup (20 g) grated Parmesan cheese

1 tbsp nori sprinkle

For the filling

¾ tbsp (10 g) unsalted butter

1 leek, trimmed and thinly sliced

2 cups (250 g) mascarpone cheese

¼ cup (50 ml) heavy whipping cream

¾ cup (100 g) hard goat cheese, crumbled

2 large eggs, beaten

0.4 oz (10 g) dried wakame, soaked for 10 minutes then shredded

sea salt

baby salad leaves, microgreens or Furikake (see page 33), to serve

Preheat the oven to 400°F (200°C). Grease a small heavy-based ovenproof pan with butter and place a circle of parchment paper in the bottom.

Put all the ingredients for the base in a food processor and blend until you have fine crumbs. Press this mixture into the bottom of the pan and set aside.

Melt the butter for the filling in a frying pan and add the leek. Cook over low-medium heat for about 5 minutes, or until soft. Season with sea salt, transfer to a mixing bowl and combine thoroughly with the mascarpone and heavy whipping cream. Add the goat cheese, beaten eggs and wakame. Fold together gently and pour into the lined pan on top of the base.

Bake for about 45 minutes, or until a skewer into the center comes out clean. Serve immediately, scattered with salad leaves, microgreens or Furikake.

SERVES 4

———

DHAL

The kombu not only adds flavor to this lentil dish, but also helps to alleviate the properties in lentils that can produce gas in the digestive system. If you do not have samphire, asparagus is a tasty alternative.

3.5 oz (100 g) dried mung beans, soaked in cold water overnight

1 tsp ground turmeric

½ tsp ground ginger

0.11 oz (3 g) strip of kombu

5½ tbsp (80 ml) canned coconut milk

1½ tbsp (20 g) unsalted butter or coconut oil

juice of 1 lime

1 tsp cumin seeds

1 tsp fennel seeds

1 tsp nigella seeds

1 tsp mustard seeds

1 cup (80 g) samphire

scant 3 cups (80 g) baby spinach

¼ cup (20 g) sea aster (optional)

good pinch of Seaweed Salt (see page 32) or sea salt

Rinse and drain the mung beans and then put them into a saucepan with 3 times their volume of water. Add the turmeric, ginger and strip of kombu. Bring to a boil, then reduce the heat and simmer for about 1 hour, or until the beans are soft. Stir through the coconut milk, take off the heat and add half the butter or coconut oil and lime juice — but don't stir through.

Melt the remaining butter or coconut oil in a frying pan over a low heat. Add the cumin, fennel, nigella and mustard seeds and stir for 2 minutes. Add the samphire, baby spinach and sea aster, if using. Stir for about 3–4 minutes, until wilted. Take off the heat, stir in the nori sprinkle and set aside.

Add a good pinch of Seaweed Salt (or use regular sea salt) to the dhal and stir to combine with the melted butter and lime juice.

Ladle the dhal into bowls and divide the spiced greens between them, then serve.

SEAWEED SLAW

Homemade coleslaw is so much fresher than store-bought varieties
that are often heavy with mayonnaise. You can also make it as
simple as you like; for example this recipe would work just as well
with just cabbage, dill, yogurt, dulse and lime.

1 large carrot

¼ white cabbage

1 large or 2 small beets

¼ cup (50 g) plain yogurt

1 tbsp dried dulse flakes

zest of 1 lime

handful of dill, finely chopped

handful of mint, finely chopped

handful of flat-leaf parsley, finely
    chopped

1 tbsp sesame seeds

sea salt

Grate or finely shred the carrot, cabbage and beets.

Combine the yogurt, dulse flakes and lime zest in a large
bowl. Add the grated vegetables and mix thoroughly until evenly coated.

Stir through the chopped herbs and sesame seeds and
season with a pinch of sea salt.

BUTTER AND SOY UMAMI POTATOES

The addition of a little soy sauce and some nori sprinkle to buttery new potatoes just makes them even more delicious. This is an instant way to add umami to any vegetable dish.

1 lb (500 g) new potatoes
2 tbsp (30 g) butter
2 garlic cloves, smashed
1 tbsp soy sauce
2 tbsp nori sprinkle

Cook the potatoes in a large saucepan of boiling water for about 10 minutes, until they are soft. Drain and leave to cool. Once cooled, lightly smash the potatoes with a fork so that they are slightly broken but still round and intact.

Place a large frying pan over a medium-high heat and melt the butter. Add the smashed garlic and fry for a minute until fragrant.

Add the potatoes and fry, stirring and coating the potatoes with the butter. Add the soy sauce and keep tossing the potatoes for another couple of minutes. Add the nori sprinkle and toss until mixed through. Serve warm or at room temperature.

SEAWEED TOFU NOODLES

The different elements of this dish work wonderfully as a whole, and also individually, so you might want to try just the tofu or make the noodles and simply add some Gomashio dusted tofu for a quick version.

1 sheet of nori

7 oz (200 g) extra-firm tofu

white wine, to cover

½ cup (100 ml) sparkling water

¾ cup (100 g) tempura flour

vegetable oil, for deep-frying

2.75 oz (80 g) noodles

1 tbsp sesame oil

1 tbsp Gomashio (see page 32) or toasted sesame seeds

½ tsp Seaweed Salt (see page 32) or sea salt

1 spring onion, sliced

1½ tbsp (40 g) Pickled Seaweed (see page 37), shredded

sea salt and black pepper

Wet the nori sheet, which will allow you to roll it easily. Wrap the tofu securely in the nori sheet, as if you were wrapping a present. Marinate the wrapped tofu in white wine overnight. The trick is to find the smallest container or bowl that the tofu will fit into so that you don't need a lot of wine to cover it.

When you are ready to cook the dish, pour the sparkling water into a bowl and add the tempura flour a little at a time, whisking continuously until you reach a thick batter-like consistency. Roll the wrapped tofu in the batter a few times so that it is nicely coated.

Being very careful, pour vegetable oil into a wok to a depth of about 1¼ inches (3 cm) and heat until the oil reaches 180°C (350°F) — if you don't have a kitchen thermometer, toss in a pinch of flour; it should sizzle immediately. Remove the wok from the heat and very gently use kitchen tongs to lower the tofu into the oil. Step back as soon as you do so and wait for it to go golden in color before gently turning it over. When it is golden on all sides, remove and drain on paper towels to absorb the excess oil.

For the broth

2 lemongrass sticks, bashed

1 tbsp tamari

Cook the noodles in a large saucepan of boiling salted water until just tender. Drain and rinse with cold water to cool quickly and drain again. Transfer to large bowl and mix in the sesame oil, Gomashio and Seaweed Salt to coat.

Meanwhile, infuse the bashed lemongrass in ½ cup (150 ml) simmering water for 10 minutes and add a splash of tamari.

To serve, divide the noodles between bowls, add some lemongrass broth and top with the sliced spring onion and Pickled Seaweed. Slice the tofu into 4 pieces and place on top of the noodles.

MACARONI AND CHEESE

This is pure, unadulterated comfort food. The addition of seaweed to the crispy topping just adds another layer of umami flavor to all the cheeses, along with the hint of mustard. If you cannot find Comté cheese, Gruyère or Emmenthal are good alternatives.

3½ tbsp (50 g) unsalted butter

generous ½ cup (250 g) panko (Japanese breadcrumbs)

4 tbsp Furikake (see page 33)

2 tsp thyme leaves

1 lb (500 g) macaroni

1 tbsp olive oil

3¼ cups (750 ml) milk

0.88 oz (25 g) kombu

3 tbsp (25 g) all-purpose flour

1⅛ cup (250 g) mascarpone cheese

2 cups (200 g) Comté cheese, grated

2 cups (200 g) Parmesan cheese, grated

2 cups (200 g) Cheddar cheese, grated

1 tsp English mustard powder

sea salt

Preheat the oven to 350°F (180°C).

Melt 2 tablespoons of butter in a saucepan. Add the panko and cook, stirring continuously, until the crumbs are golden brown. Remove from the pan and place on paper towels to absorb the excess oil before transferring to a small bowl. Toss with the Furikake and thyme leaves.

Cook the pasta in a large saucepan of boiling salted water until al dente. Drain and toss in a little olive oil to prevent sticking. Put the milk and kombu in a small saucepan and bring to a gentle simmer. Remove from the heat, discard the kombu and season with a little salt. Set aside.

Melt 1½ tablespoons of butter in a saucepan. Stir in the flour and cook the mixture for just under a minute; this is known as a roux. Add the hot milk to the roux, a little at a time, stirring continuously to avoid lumps. Bring the mixture to a boil, stirring constantly, until thick and glossy. Add all the cheeses and the mustard powder and stir until the cheeses are melted and the sauce is smooth. Remove from heat and mix the cheese sauce with the pasta in a large bowl before transferring to a baking dish.

Bake in the oven for 10 minutes, then top with the fried breadcrumbs and bake for a further 10–15 minutes until the sauce is bubbling around the edges. Leave to cool for 10 minutes before serving.

GNOCCHI
WITH SEAWEED PESTO

This seaweed pesto is equally good with linguine or spinach and ricotta tortellini. Gnocchi are a bit of a fiddle to make, but always worth the effort.

For the gnocchi

1 tbsp rock salt

1½ lbs (700 g) Russet potatoes

6 cups (200 g) baby spinach leaves

drizzle of olive oil

1½ cups (200 g) all-purpose flour, sifted

2 eggs, beaten

1 tsp sea salt

1 tbsp (20 g) unsalted butter

4 tbsp toasted pumpkin seeds, to serve

chopped mixed herbs (basil, parsley, chives), to garnish

Preheat the oven to 425°F (220°C).

Scatter the rock salt over a sheet pan, place the potatoes on top and bake for about 45 minutes, or until easily pierced with a sharp knife. When just cool enough to handle, peel the potatoes and run them through a potato ricer into a bowl. (Alternatively, mash the potatoes and then press through a strainer). Leave to cool.

Puree the baby spinach in a blender with a little olive oil. Add to the potatoes and combine thoroughly, then add the flour, eggs and salt and mix together. Gather the dough together and place on a floured surface. Knead gently until all the flour is all incorporated. It should be slightly sticky.

Cut the dough into 4 equal pieces. Roll each piece into a sausage-like shape and cut into equal-sized gnocchi. Use a fork, if you like, to mark each one with indentations and then set aside to rest for 20–30 minutes before cooking.

Boil the gnocchi in batches in a large saucepan of salted water. They are ready when they have fully come to the surface. Remove with a slotted spoon and drain on paper towels as you cook the next batch.

For the seaweed pesto

generous 2 tbsp (20 g) pine nuts

scant ½ cup (20 g) mixed dried
seaweed flakes

2½ cups (60 g) fresh basil leaves

4 tbsp (20 g) Parmesan cheese,
grated

1–2 tsp olive oil

freshly ground black pepper

For the pesto, toast the pine nuts in a dry frying pan over a low heat until lightly colored. Place all the ingredients in a blender (or use a pestle and mortar) and puree until you get the required consistency.

To serve, heat the butter in a large frying pan over medium heat, add the gnocchi and sear on both sides. Place a generous spoonful of seaweed pesto on each plate. Scatter the gnocchi over the pesto and sprinkle with toasted pumpkin seeds and garnish with any fresh herbs you have on hand.

FURIKAKE FETA AND TOMATO SALAD

This quick salad is beautiful and full of fresh flavors. The vine leaves are optional, but do add a lovely crunch. We discovered that nori furikake and feta go together brilliantly — all that natural saltiness cuts through the sweet tomatoes.

7 oz (200 g) feta, drained and cubed

2 tbsp Furikake (*see* page 33)

4 tbsp pumpkin seeds

1 lb (500 g) mixed heritage tomatoes

2 tbsp Seaweed Oil (*see* page 33) or extra virgin olive oil

For the crispy vine leaves (optional)

6–8 vine leaves

sunflower oil, for frying

In a bowl, toss the feta in the Furikake.

Toast the pumpkin seeds in a dry frying pan over medium heat until they begin to color.

For the crispy vine leaves, if using, heat the sunflower oil in a frying pan and when hot fry the leaves until crispy.

Arrange the tomatoes and feta in a serving dish and scatter over the pumpkin seeds and crispy vine leaves. Drizzle with Seaweed Oil.

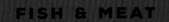

FISH & MEAT

SEA BREAM
WITH NORI BUTTER AND SEA SPAGHETTI

Nori butter is a wonderful way to add a finish to any pan-fried fish.
It's also delicious melted over new potatoes. Sea spaghetti is the
common name for a type of seaweed also known as thongweed
or buttonweed that naturally looks like spaghetti. If sea bream is
unavailable, red snapper and sea bass are good alternatives.

0.7 oz (20 g) seaweed spaghetti (dried weight), soaked in water for 1 hour

½ Napa cabbage, sliced

2 tbsp olive oil

2 sea bream fillets

1 tbsp (20 g) unsalted butter

1 tsp nori sprinkle

1½ cups (40 g) baby Chinese greens (or use baby spinach)

sea salt

To serve

purple shiso leaves (or basil)

coriander leaves

squeeze of lemon juice

Drain the seaweed spaghetti, then steam with the Napa cabbage for 10 minutes. Set aside.

Heat the olive oil in a nonstick frying pan over medium heat and season the sea bream generously with sea salt. When the oil is nice and hot lay the fillets skin side down in the pan. Don't be tempted to move the fillets around too much. Cook without turning for 5–7 minutes until the skin is crispy and golden and the white flesh is almost cooked through.

Add half the butter to the pan, take off the heat and gently flip over the fillets, spooning the melted butter over the fish. After about 30 seconds, remove the fillets and set aside.

Add the remaining butter and nori sprinkle to the same pan and bring up the heat again. Add the steamed sea spaghetti and cabbage and heat through, making sure the nori butter covers all the vegetables.

Arrange the seaweed spaghetti and cabbage on two plates, along with the baby Chinese greens. Top with the sea bream fillets, then scatter over some purple shiso. Serve sprinkled with coriander leaves, lemon juice and pinch of sea salt.

POKE BOWL

Poke bowls are from Hawaii and are often made with raw fish, but here we've created a bowl with prawns, brown rice and pickled radishes. The crispy nori on the side adds the traditional crunch found in a poke bowl. If juniper berries are not available, add 2 tbsp of a good quality gin, which has no additional flavoring. Alternatively, use a medium-sized sprig of fresh rosemary.

scant ¼ cup (50 ml) rice vinegar

1 tbsp brown sugar

1 tsp toasted sesame seeds

1 tsp juniper berries, crushed

scant ¼ cup (50 ml) water

5 red radishes, thinly sliced

¾ cup + 1½ tbsp (160 g) brown rice

2 tbsp tamari

1 tbsp fish sauce

1 tsp toasted sesame oil

7 oz (200 g) raw prawns, shelled and deveined

1 nori sheet, cut into triangles, to serve

chopped mixed herbs, to serve

crispy fish skin, to serve (optional)

Put the vinegar, sugar, sesame seeds and juniper berries and water into a small saucepan and bring to a simmer over a medium-high heat. Cook, stirring occasionally for about 2 minutes, until the sugar has dissolved.

Pour this pickling liquid immediately over the radishes in a bowl and leave to cool. Cover and chill for at least 2 hours.

Meanwhile, rinse the brown rice until the water runs clear. Cook according to instructions, drain and toss in the tamari, fish sauce and sesame oil. Cover and leave to rest but keep warm.

Bring a saucepan of water to a boil and season generously with salt. Add the prawns, cover and remove from the heat. Check if the prawns are cooked through after 3 minutes (they should be no longer translucent). Drain and toss with the radishes and a little of the pickling liquid. Divide the rice between bowls and top with the prawns and radishes. Add the nori triangles on the side and garnish with a few herbs (we used chive flowers, thyme and chopped parsley).

SALMON TEMPURA ROLLS

These rolls are quite simple to make once you get the hang of folding in the edges of the nori sheet and rolling it nice and tight. The tempura batter is lovely and light and is great for vegetables, too.

1 nori sheet

¼ lb (100 g) poached salmon, flaked into bite-sized pieces

½ cup (100 ml) sodium-free sparkling water

⅓ cup (40 g) tempura flour

vegetable oil for frying

Seaweed Tartar Sauce (see page 43), to serve

chive flowers, to serve (optional)

Wet the nori sheet and arrange the flaked salmon in a line along the center of the sheet but not quite to the edges. Fold both edges into the center and then roll into a tight roll.

Pour the sparkling water into a bowl and add the tempura flour, a little at a time, whisking continuously until you reach a thick batter-like consistency. Dip the roll a few times into the tempura batter.

Pour vegetable oil into a wok to a depth of about ¾ inch (2 cm) and place over a medium-high heat until the oil reaches 180°C (350°F). (If you don't have a kitchen thermometer, toss in a pinch of flour; it should sizzle immediately.) Carefully remove the wok from the heat and use kitchen tongs to lower the roll into the hot oil. Turn gently until golden on all sides, then remove from the wok and drain on paper towels.

Slice into 4 pieces and serve with some Seaweed Tartar Sauce, garnished with a few chive flowers, if desired.

CLAM LINGUINE

This is a slightly different take on seafood pasta, not least because it has dulse but also dill and onion jam! But when you combine all these flavors together, they make an unexpected and delicious bowl of pasta.

2 red onions, 1 thickly sliced and 1 finely chopped

1 tbsp coconut oil

1 tbsp pomegranate molasses

9 oz (250 g) linguini

1 tbsp (20 g) unsalted butter

10 oz (300 g) clams, rinsed thoroughly

zest of 1 lemon

2 tbsp fish sauce

4 tbsp (30 g) dill, chopped

2 tbsp dried dulse flakes

herb flowers, to garnish

Preheat the oven to 250°F (120°C).

Put the sliced onion, coconut oil and pomegranate molasses into a small ovenproof dish and cook in the oven for 1 hour. Remove from the oven and set aside.

Cook the linguini in a large saucepan of boiling salted water until al dente, or according to the instructions on the package.

Meanwhile, place a large, lidded frying pan over medium heat, add half the butter and the chopped onion, and sauté for about 5 minutes.

Increase the heat and add the clams to the frying pan along with the lemon zest and fish sauce. Cover and cook for about 3–4 minutes, until all the clams have opened, discarding any closed ones, then add the remaining butter. Remove from the heat and set aside.

Drain the pasta and while hot stir in the chopped dill and the onion jam. Divide between shallow bowls. Sprinkle the dulse flakes over the pasta and top with the clams. Garnish with whatever herb flowers you have on hand.

SEAWEED GIN-CURED SALMON

This recipe is simple but takes a bit of time, which is what
makes it special and perfect for when you have friends for
dinner or lunch in the garden.

1 lb (500 g) salmon fillet in one piece, skin on

zest of 1 lime

1 tsp black peppercorns, crushed in a pestle and mortar

⅓ cup (100 g) sea salt flakes

⅓ cup (100 g) coconut sugar or raw cane sugar

⅓ cup (80 ml) dry gin, infused with 0.7 oz (20 g) kombu overnight

buttered brown bread and sliced cucumber, to serve

Remove any pin bones from the salmon fillet.

Mix all the remaining ingredients together in a bowl. Spread half this mixture over the base of a non-metallic dish that is large enough to hold the salmon. Put the salmon on top, skin side down, and cover with the remaining curing mixture so that the salmon is completely covered. Cover the dish with plastic wrap and leave overnight in the refrigerator.

Remove the salmon from the cure, rinse and gently pat dry with paper towels.

To serve, thinly slice the salmon and serve with buttered brown bread and sliced cucumber.

CRAB CONGEE

Congee is a Chinese way of cooking rice for a long period of time so that it breaks down into a soupy consistency. It looks odd when you first try it, but it makes a wonderful base for so many combinations of toppings. Here the rice is cooked with kombu. Swap the crab for tofu for a vegetarian version.

generous ⅓ cup (80 g) short-grain rice

0.7 oz (20 g) dried kombu, soaked for 20 minutes

thumb-sized piece of fresh ginger root, sliced into discs

sea salt

To serve

1.75 oz (50 g) white and brown crab meat

1 tbsp black or white sesame seeds

fresh ginger, peeled and cut into thin matchsticks

4 radishes, thinly sliced

2 spring onions, thinly sliced

nori strips

toasted sesame oil

Seaweed Aioli (optional, *see* page 42)

Put the rice into a large saucepan with 7 times its volume of cold water. Add the kombu and sliced ginger and bring to a boil, then reduce the heat and simmer gently for about 1½ hours until the rice has broken down into a gloopy consistency. Take off the heat and remove and discard the ginger slices.

To serve, ladle the congee into 2 bowls and top with crab meat, sesame seeds, ginger, radishes, spring onion and a few crispy nori strips. Drizzle over a little toasted sesame oil, a pinch of salt and a spoonful of Seaweed Aioli, if using.

LAMB MARINATED
WITH SEAWEED

This is a recipe that uses seaweed and leftover pickling liquid to brine meat, which makes it wonderfully tender, flavorsome and easy to cook.

½ cup + 2 tbsp (150 ml) pickling liquid (*see* page 41)

2 pieces of kombu, each large enough to wrap a steak

2 lamb leg steaks

1 nori sheet, halved

2 tsp olive oil

Seaweed Salt (*see* page 32)

200 g broccolini

1 radicchio, quartered

purple basil, to garnish (optional)

Gomashio (*see* page 32), to garnish (optional)

For the miso dressing

1 tbsp sugar

1 tbsp miso paste

1 tsp sake

1 tsp mirin

1 tbsp yuzu or lemon juice

scant ½ cup (100 ml) buttermilk

Bring the pickling liquid to a boil in a small saucepan. Once boiling, add the kombu pieces, remove from the heat and set aside until the kombu has softened.

Wrap each steak first with nori and then kombu and place in a small container or bowl. Allow the pickling liquid to cool and then pour over the wrapped steaks so that the meat is covered by the liquid. Leave to marinate in the fridge overnight.

To cook the steaks, remove from the pickling liquid and unwrap (discard the kombu, nori and liquid). Pat dry with paper towels and rub with a little olive oil. Place a grill pan over high heat; when very hot add the steaks and sear for 2 minutes on each side for medium-rare, longer for well done. (The steaks will cook quickly because they have been brined.) Take out of the pan and rest on a meat board, seasoning with a little Seaweed Salt.

In the same pan, grill the broccoli until it looks charred, then remove from the pan and repeat with the radicchio. Meanwhile, whisk all the dressing ingredients together.

Place the broccoli and radicchio in the center of two plates and top with sliced lamb. Drizzle with a little dressing and garnish with purple basil and Gomashio, if using.

SEAWEED PANKO CHICKEN

This is a delicious "crumb" recipe that you can also use for oven baking chicken or fish, or pan frying if you don't feel confident with deep-frying.

4 small or 2 large boneless, skinless chicken thighs (halved)

mixed salad leaves, to serve

Seaweed Slaw (see page 64), to serve

garden cress or micro herbs, to serve (optional)

For the brine

1 tsp brown mustard seeds

1 tsp cumin seeds

1 tsp fennel seeds

scant ½ cup (100 g) sea salt

½ cup (100 g) light brown sugar

1 tsp black peppercorns

2 bay leaves

For the crumb

1 tbsp sesame seeds

1 tsp ground fennel

1 tbsp wakame, very finely chopped in a blender

¾ cup + 2 tbsp (80 g) panko or breadcrumbs

2 large eggs

¾ cup + 2 tbsp (100 g) all-purpose flour

vegetable oil, for deep-frying

Mix all brine ingredients together and use to cover the chicken pieces. Set aside in the refrigerator for 2 hours, turning them over after 1 hour. Wash the brine off the chicken and pat dry with paper towels.

To make the crumb, mix together the sesame seeds, fennel, wakame and panko crumbs. Whisk the eggs in a separate bowl and put the flour into a shallow bowl.

Working with one piece at a time, place the chicken first in flour, then egg and finally the crumb. Do this twice for each piece and place on a wire rack.

Pour enough vegetable oil into a large saucepan to come halfway up the sides. Heat the oil until it reaches 350°F (180°C). If you don't have a kitchen thermometer you can test the temperature by adding a pinch of breadcrumbs; they should sizzle immediately. Gently lower in 2 pieces of chicken, one at a time, and fry for about 8–10 minutes, turning often with tongs, until a deep golden brown. Transfer the chicken to clean wire racks and leave to rest for 10 minutes. Please do this step with utmost care, moving away from the direct heat when you see the oil is getting too hot. Repeat with the remaining pieces of chicken.

Serve with salad leaves, Seaweed Slaw and micro herbs, if using.

———

STEAK
WITH SEAWEED RELISH

Here is a quick recipe using the Seaweed Relish in the Condiments & Snacks chapter. It's great to have ideas on hand for using up recipes and this butter is incredible with steak.

---

10 oz (300 g) rib-eye steak

Seaweed Salt (*see* page 32)

½ pound (200 g) new potatoes, scrubbed

1 tsp olive oil

generous tbsp (30 g) Seaweed Relish (*see* page 37)

butter and sea salt, for the potatoes

2½ cups (80 g) fresh watercress, to serve

Remove the steak from the fridge about an hour before you want to cook it to bring it to room temperature. Season on both sides with Seaweed Salt.

Meanwhile, put the potatoes in a saucepan, cover with plenty of cold water and bring to a boil. Reduce the heat and simmer until cooked but still with a little bite — depending on your potatoes this will take about 10–15 minutes.

Heat a grill pan and when very hot, add the olive oil to the pan. Wait for the oil to become really hot and then place the steak in the center of the pan. Cook for about 4 minutes on each side for medium rare, a little longer if you prefer your steak well done.

Add the Seaweed Relish to the top of the cooked steak and remove the pan from the heat. Transfer to a board to rest for about 8 minutes (the same amount of time as you cooked the steak). Meanwhile, drain the new potatoes and dress with a little butter and sea salt.

To serve, slice the steak into strips and serve with buttery new potatoes and watercress.

TERIYAKI CHICKEN BURGER

We've suggested burger buns for this teriyaki grilled chicken,
but it would go equally well with fresh vegetables, rice or
noodles. Chicken will never be boring again.

2 boneless skinless chicken
    thighs
1 large spring onion, thinly sliced
    at an angle
1 nori sheet, cut in half
2 brioche burger buns
2–4 lettuce leaves, washed and
    patted dry

For the teriyaki sauce
2 tbsp soy sauce
2 tbsp cooking sake
2 tbsp mirin
1 tbsp soft light brown sugar
1 strip of kombu
    (about 0.35 oz /10 g)

Make the teriyaki sauce by combining all the ingredients
in a small saucepan and bringing to a boil, stirring
continuously. Once it comes to a boil and the sugar
has dissolved, reduce the heat and simmer the sauce
for 10 minutes, or until thickened to the consistency of
molasses. Take off the heat and leave to cool, removing
the kombu.

Put the chicken thighs in a bowl and add some of the
cooled teriyaki sauce, just enough to coat them. Leave
to marinate for 2 hours.

Preheat the grill to high. Grill the chicken thighs for
5 – 7 minutes on each side, or until the chicken is completely cooked through.

Remove from the tray, glaze each chicken thigh with a
little more teriyaki sauce then sprinkle with the spring
onions. Once coated with spring onions, wrap each thigh
in a half sheet of nori and arrange in the burger buns
with the lettuce on top. Serve warm.

SEVEN-SPICE PORK

This dish is packed with flavor and if you make extra
it's perfect for delicious leftovers the following day.
Shichimi togarashi is a Japanese blend of seven
spices — it has a kick so add to your own taste.

---

vegetable oil, for frying

1¾ lbs (800 g) pork shoulder, cut into ¾ inch (2 cm) cubes

4 shallots, chopped

2 garlic cloves, chopped

½–1 tbsp shichimi togarashi (Japanese seven-spice powder)

1 tbsp nori sprinkle

⅓ cup (80 ml) ponzu

1¾ tbsp (40 g) coconut sugar or raw cane sugar

4 tbsp fish sauce

1¼ cups (240 g) brown rice

7 oz (200 g) asparagus tips

olive oil, for drizzling

sea salt

crispy onions, to serve (optional)

Heat a little oil in a large, heavy-based frying pan or wok over medium-high heat. Add the pork in batches and brown on all sides. Remove from the pan with a slotted spoon and set aside.

Heat a little more oil in the pan, add the shallots and garlic and cook for about 5 minutes. Stir in the shichimi togarashi and nori sprinkle. Continue to cook for a couple of minutes to release the flavors.

Return the pork to the pan and stir. Add a scant 1¾ cups (400 ml) water, the ponzu, coconut sugar and fish sauce. Bring to a simmer, then cover with a lid and simmer over a low heat for about 1 hour.

Meanwhile, cook the rice according to the package instructions. Just before the pork is ready, place a grill pan over high heat, drizzle in a little olive oil and add the asparagus tips. Season with sea salt.

Drain the rice, add to the pan of pork and mix through before ladling into deep bowls. Serve with the grilled asparagus tips and top with some crispy onions for a bit of crunch, if desired.

DESSERTS

VEGAN SUPERFOOD CAKE

Adding seaweed flakes to a cake might seem rather strange at first, but sweet often needs a little savory to really bring out the flavors. This is a super easy cake that you can dress up when you serve and surprise any friend, vegan or otherwise.

4 tbsp flaxseed, finely ground

½ cup (120 ml) warm water

¾ cup + 1 tbsp (170 g) coconut oil, melted

1 cup (230 g) soft light brown sugar

1 tsp ground cinnamon

1½ cups + 2½ tbsp (240 g) all-purpose flour or gluten-free flour

½ cup (60 g) ground almonds

1 tbsp baking powder

½ tsp sea salt

3 tbsp nori sprinkle, plus extra to serve

1 cup (235 ml) full-fat coconut milk

1 cup (100 g) blueberries

½ cup (100 g) pomegranate seeds, plus extra to serve

vegan coconut yogurt, to serve

Preheat the oven to 325°F (170°C). Grease and line a 9 inch (23 cm) springform cake pan with parchment paper.

In a small bowl, combine the ground flaxseed and water, mix and leave for 5 minutes to swell up.

Meanwhile, cream the coconut oil and sugar in a large bowl with a whisk for a few minutes until well mixed.

Add the flaxseed mixture, sugar, cinnamon, flour, ground almonds, baking powder, sea salt and nori sprinkles, and mix well. Gently mix in the coconut milk and lastly fold in the blueberries and pomegranate seeds.

Pour into the lined pan and smooth the surface. Bake for 45 minutes, or until a skewer inserted into the center comes out clean. Remove from the pan and leave to cool on a wire rack.

Serve with fresh pomegranate seeds, vegan coconut yogurt and nori sprinkle. The cake can be stored in an airtight container for up to 3 days.

FRUIT CRUMBLE

As both rhubarb and apples are considered a good
flavor match for the umami notes of seaweed, a
crumble seems the perfect choice for dessert.

For the fruit filling

1½ large (300 g) Honeycrisp
  apple, peeled, cored and
  diced

1 tbsp kelp powder

1 tsp ground cinnamon

generous ⅓ cup (60 g) coconut
  sugar

1 large (50 g) rhubarb stalk,
  trimmed and chopped

For the topping

1 cup (100 g) rolled oats

¼ cup (60 g) muscovado sugar

scant ½ cup (50 g) ground
  almonds

2 tbsp brown rice flour

1 tsp kelp powder

¼ tsp grated nutmeg

2 tbsp coconut oil

½ cup (75 g) chopped hazelnuts

custard or Greek yogurt, to serve

Preheat the oven to 350°F (180°C).

To make the fruit filling, put the diced apple, kelp powder,
cinnamon and half of the coconut sugar in a wide-bottomed saucepan and cook over a low heat, stirring often.
When the sugar has dissolved and the apples have caramelized and begun to soften, add the rest of the sugar and
the rhubarb. Cook for another couple of minutes until the
rhubarb has also begun to soften. Transfer to an ovenproof dish and set aside.

To make the crumble, combine the oats, sugar, ground almonds, flour, kelp powder and nutmeg in a bowl. Add the
coconut oil and combine until the mixture resembles
clumpy breadcrumbs. Stir in the hazelnuts.

Add the topping to the fruit filling and bake for about 30
minutes until the top is golden and the filling is beginning to bubble through.

Serve with your favorite custard or some Greek yogurt.

CHERRY AND DULSE BROWNIES

Cherries and dulse make an unlikely but happy
couple in these dark, chocolaty brownies. Equally,
prunes would work well too.

½ cup (125 g) unsalted butter

1.75 oz (50 g) dark chocolate

1⅛ cup (225 g) light muscovado sugar

½ cup (50 g) cocoa powder

¾ cup + 2 tbsp (100 g) all-purpose flour

1 tsp baking powder

3 eggs, beaten

scant cup (200 g) cherries, pitted and halved

1 tbsp dried dulse flakes

Preheat the oven to 350°F (180ºC). Line an 8 inch (20 cm) square baking pan with parchment paper.

Melt the butter, dark chocolate and sugar together in a saucepan, stirring until thoroughly combined and the sugar has dissolved, then remove from the heat.

Sift the cocoa powder, flour and baking powder into a bowl. Pour in the melted butter and chocolate and mix to fully combine. Gradually beat in the eggs until you have a smooth, shiny consistency. Stir in the cherries and dulse flakes.

Pour the mixture into the lined pan and bake for about 20–25 minutes until set but still with a bit of give in the center. Remove from the oven and leave to cool in the pan for 5 minutes, then turn out on to a wire rack to cool completely. Cut into 16 squares to serve.

SEAWEED COOKIES

Just as salt is being used to complement chocolate or caramel,
the saltiness of the seaweed in these shortbread cookies goes
wonderfully with the sweet butter crunchiness.

½ cup (100 g) unsalted butter, softened, plus extra for greasing

¼ cup (50 g) *superfine sugar, plus extra for sprinkling

¾ cup + 2 tbsp (100 g) all-purpose flour, plus extra for dusting

½ cup (50 g) cornstarch

1 tsp dried dulse flakes

pinch of salt

Lightly butter a sheet pan.

Put the butter and sugar in a large bowl and use a wooden spoon or hand mixer to cream until light and fluffy.

Sift the flour and cornstarch into another bowl and mix in the dulse flakes and salt until completely combined. Add this to the butter and sugar and mix everything together until smooth. Tip this mixture out onto a lightly floured surface and knead gently to form a dough.

Roll out the dough to a thickness of about ⅓ inch (1 cm) and use a cookie cutter to cut out cookies. Place them on the buttered sheet pan and chill on the tray for about 30 minutes. Meanwhile, preheat the oven to 350°F (180°C).

Bake the cookies for 20 minutes, then take out of the oven and leave for a few minutes before transferring to a wire rack and sprinkling with more sugar. Keep in an airtight container for up to 3 days.

*Superfine sugar is not to be confused with icing sugar. If you can't find superfine sugar, you can pulse regular sugar in a blender or food processor for a similar consistency.

———

ELDERFLOWER AND SUMMER BERRY GELATIN

Agar agar is a natural gelling agent extracted from red algae and is a great vegetarian alternative to gelatin when making jelly. These desserts are wonderful for a special summer occasion.

sunflower oil, for greasing
2 cups (500 ml) water
1 tbsp (5 g) agar agar flakes
2–4 tbsp elderflower cordial
⅓ cup (80 g) superfine sugar
10–16 blueberries
4 strawberries, hulled and cut in half
8–12 edible flowers (such as violas, nasturtiums and elderflowers)
Furikake (see page 33), to serve

Lightly grease 8 holes of a muffin pan with sunflower oil.

Put the water in a small saucepan and pour the agar flakes on top, whisking gently. Slowly bring the water to a boil; once it reaches a boil, whisk continuously for 5 minutes. Then turn the heat off and add the sugar and cordial, stirring until dissolved. Remove from the heat.

Pour a small amount of this liquid into each muffin hole to a depth of about ¼ inch (5 mm). Keep the pan on a warm stovetop while the base starts to set; this should take about 3–5 minutes at room temperature.

Arrange the berries and edible flowers on the first layer as desired. Pour the rest of the liquid into each hole, filling it to near the top.

The desserts will fully set at room temperature in about 10–15 minutes or in less time in the fridge. Once they are set they can easily be twisted out of the molds and kept in an airtight container for a week. These have a much higher melting point than normal gelatin desserts and so can be left out at room temperature for longer. To serve, sprinkle with some Furikake.

SALTED CARAMEL AND SEAWEED POPCORN

Salted caramel and seaweed appears to be a match made in heaven; the only difficulty with this recipe is stopping yourself from eating the whole bowl.

2 tbsp coconut oil, melted

4 tbsp (50 g) popcorn kernels

For the salted caramel

scant ½ cup (110 g) golden
  superfine sugar

2 tbsp maple or corn syrup

2 tbsp (25 g) unsalted butter

½ tsp sea salt

2 tbsp sesame seeds

3 sheets (5 g) nori, torn up into
  small pieces

Heat the oil in a large saucepan that has a lid. Add the kernels and cover, keeping the heat to medium. In a couple of minutes the corn will start to pop. With the lid on, shake the pot occasionally to encourage the unpopped kernels to pop and prevent burning.

Once the popping sounds become few and far between, take the pan off the heat, pour the popcorn into a bowl and set aside.

Place a sheet of parchment paper on the work surface (this is for the caramelized popcorn). The caramel will set quite quickly once the popcorn is added at the end so try to work quickly.

To make the caramel, place the saucepan over medium heat for 1 minute. Add the sugar and the maple or corn syrup to the middle of the pan. Without stirring, wait for the sugar to melt and turn a light brown color.

At this point, reduce the heat and add the butter and salt, stirring with a wooden spoon or rubber spatula until it all combines. Be careful as the hot caramel may spit initially. Quickly add the sesame seeds and nori and stir through. Finally toss all the popcorn into the pan and

try to mix until the popcorn is fully coated in the caramel. This step is easier to do on the warm stovetop to prevent the caramel from setting as quickly.

Once the popcorn is coated, pour on to your sheet of parchment paper. While the popcorn will be quite hot at this stage, you may be able to separate the corn with nimble fingers so it isn't all clumped together. Once fully cooled, keep the popcorn in an airtight container for up to a month.

DRINKS

———

TEA

Kelp tea is a traditional tea in Japan and Korea made by infusing kelp seaweed in hot water. In Japan, where it is called *konbu-cha*, it is considered an all-round tonic. Bladderwrack seaweed is also thought to make a type of tea that is particularly good for the digestion, especially when combined with mint. However, an easier way to start drinking seaweed is to mix a few dulse flakes into green leaf tea.

2 tsp green leaf tea
¼ tsp dried dulse flakes

Warm a teapot with just-boiled water and then discard the water.

Add the green tea and dulse to the pot. Wait for about 5 minutes after boiling the water to fill the pot.

Steep for 2–3 minutes and pour through a tea strainer.

DULSE DIGESTIVE SMOOTHIE

Pineapple, celery and cucumber are all excellent for the digestion, while hemp oil is high in essential fatty acids (walnut or flaxseeds oils are good alternatives) and will keep you feeling fuller for longer.

½ cup (100 g) fresh pineapple, chopped

2 celery sticks, chopped

⅓ cucumber, chopped

2 tbsp lime juice

1 tbsp hemp oil

½ tsp dried dulse flakes

ice cubes (optional)

Put all the ingredients into a blender and blend until completely smooth.

Add ice cubes if desired and water if you like a thinner consistency.

GREEN SMOOTHIE

Kelp powder and dulse flakes are the easiest forms of seaweed to add
to your morning smoothie. Just half a teaspoon of either will give
you a fantastic mineral boost.

1 avocado, peeled and pitted

handful of baby spinach

⅓ cucumber, roughly chopped

½ frozen banana

squeeze of lemon juice

½ tsp kelp powder

generous ½ cup (100 ml) coconut
water, plus extra if needed

couple of ice cubes

Put all the smoothie ingredients into a blender and
blend until smooth.

Add more coconut water for a thinner consistency.

IRISH MOSS DRINK

This is a vegan version of a recipe from Jamaica for Irish moss (carrageen) drink, considered to be a tonic. Irish moss is a species of red algae and is more commonly known for its thickening properties. It can be found where Caribbean and Latin American specialty foods are sold.

0.14 oz (4 g) Irish moss

2¼ cups (500 ml) water

1 cinnamon stick

good pinch of grated nutmeg

1 vanilla pod

2¼ cups (500 ml) coconut milk

2 tbsp maple syrup

ground cinnamon or grated nutmeg, to serve

Cover the Irish moss with water in a bowl and leave it to soak for 1 hour before draining and rinsing thoroughly.

Pour the water into a saucepan, add the cinnamon stick and nutmeg and bring to a boil. Split the vanilla pod and scrape out the seeds with the tip of your knife, adding to the water. Once boiling, add the Irish moss and simmer for about 1 minute. Take off the heat, cover and leave to stand for 1 hour before straining.

Combine the Irish moss mixture with the coconut milk and maple syrup in a jar with a tight-fitting lid. Close the lid and give the mixture a really good shake until thick and creamy.

You can serve either over ice or warmed through, with a dusting of cinnamon or nutmeg.

———

BLOODY MARY

Make these for the perfect Sunday brunch,
with or without the vodka.

Seaweed Salt (*see* page 32)

4 handfuls of ice

1 cup (200 ml) vodka

3⅓ cups (800 ml) tomato juice

2 tbsp lemon juice

4 tsp Worcestershire sauce

½ tsp Tabasco sauce (or more, to taste)

To serve

dried dulse flakes

pomegranate seeds (optional)

4 celery sticks

Dip the rims of four glasses in the Seaweed Salt and divide the ice among the glasses.

In a large jug, combine the vodka, tomato juice, lemon juice, Worcestershire sauce and Tabasco sauce to taste.

Pour into the glasses over the ice. Scatter over a few dulse flakes and pomegranate seeds, if using, and serve each one with a celery stick.

SEAWEED SAKE COCKTAIL

This is a tall drink for those who are less drawn to sweet cocktails.
It's very refreshing — you may want more than one! Adjust the
amount of sake to your own taste.

0.35 oz (10 g) dried kombu

1⅛ cup (250 ml) sake

½ cucumber

ice

2¼ cups (500 ml) ginger beer or
  ginger ale

In a jug, infuse the kombu in the sake for 10 minutes.
Meanwhile, peel the cucumber and set the peel aside to
serve. Slice the cucumber.

Remove the kombu from the sake and add the cucumber slices. Muddle together with the handle of a wooden
spoon so that the cucumber infuses the sake.

Add a handful of ice to each glass. Strain the sake through
a tea strainer into the glasses and top up with ginger beer.
Garnish with strips of cucumber peel, if desired.

———

SEAWEED AND LIME GIN AND TONIC

If you prefer a shorter drink, you can omit the tonic and go for a gimlet-style gin and lime. The seaweed adds just a note of savory that goes well with the botanical nature of gin.

ice

2 tbsp (30 ml) gin

2 tbsp (30 ml) lime cordial (*see below*)

tonic water

lime wedge, to serve

For the lime cordial

4 cups (1 l) water

1 lb (500 g) caster sugar

juice of 8 limes

0.7 oz (20 g) kombu

First, make the cordial. Put all the ingredients in a saucepan, bring to a boil and then reduce the heat and simmer for 15 minutes, stirring until the sugar has dissolved. Remove and discard the seaweed. Strain the cordial into sterilized bottles and keep for up to a month in the refrigerator (you should have about 4 cups (1 l) of cordial).

To make the cocktail, half-fill a glass with ice and add the gin. Add the cordial and then top up with tonic water. Add the lime wedge and use a cocktail stirrer to mix.

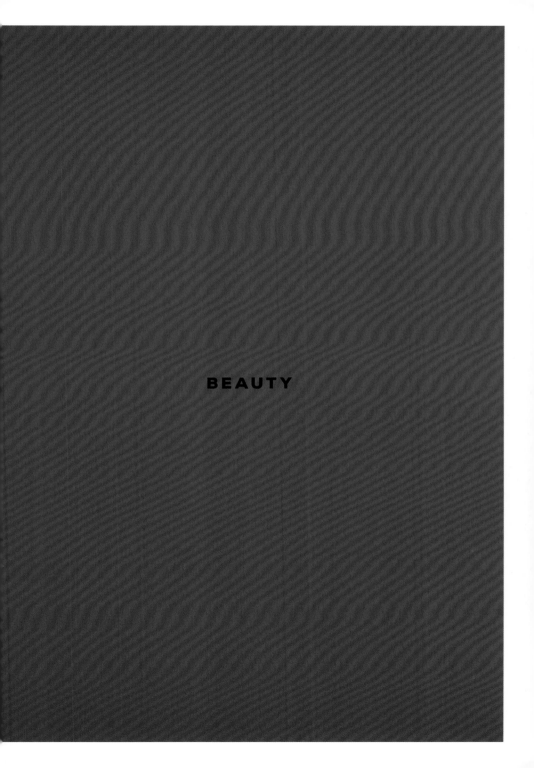

BEAUTY

SEAWEED FACE MASK

Seaweed can do wonders for winter skin, so treat
yourself to this nourishing face mask every couple of
weeks through the colder months.

1 tbsp kelp powder

½ tbsp bentonite clay (available online)

1 tsp honey

½ tsp evening primrose oil

Mix together all the ingredients with a non-metallic spoon, adding enough cold water until you have the perfect face mask consistency.

Apply generously to clean skin, avoiding the eye area, and leave for 10–15 minutes.

Rinse off with lukewarm water and a clean facecloth and pat dry. Moisturize as normal.

SEAWEED SALT SCRUB

This salt scrub is excellent for exfoliating the
skin, while the avocado oil will lock in moisture,
so that you will feel soft and revitalized.

¾ cup (200 g) sea salt

3½ tbsp (50 ml) avocado oil

2 tbsp kelp powder

10 drops of lemongrass essential
oil

10 drops of rosemary essential oil

Mix all the ingredients together with a non-metallic
spoon and store in an airtight jar.

To use, wet your skin in the shower, then step aside from
the water flow. Use a spoon or scoop to take a handful
of the scrub out of the jar (so you don't get the remaining scrub wet) and gently rub all over the skin. Simply
shower off.

Alternatively, you can use this as a hand or foot scrub.
Simply rub into damp hands or feet and rinse off.

SEAWEED BODY SCRUB

Your skin will thank you for this scrub, which is so easy to make.
We've used seagrass oil because it has an uplifting, coastal scent; if
you can't find it simply replace with your favorite essential oil.

⅔ (100 g) ground almonds

¾ cup + 2tbsp (80 g) rolled oats,
processed to a coarse powder

2½ tsp (10 g) kelp powder

3½ tsp (10 g) bentonite clay
(available online)

20 drops of seagrass essential
oil (available online)

Mix together all the ingredients with a non-metallic
spoon and store in an airtight jar.

To use, wet your skin in the shower, then step aside from
the water flow. Use a spoon or scoop to take a handful
of the scrub out of the jar (so you don't get the remaining scrub wet) and gently rub all over the skin. Simply
shower off.

BATH SOAK

Thalassotherapy (from the Greek word *thalassa*, meaning "sea") is the medical use of seaweed, seawater and shore climate as a form of therapy. The nutrients in seaweed help increase alkaline levels in the bloodstream, in turn reducing acidity levels in the body and the skin. Seaweed is also an excellent natural source of omega-3 fatty acids that promote healthy skin. Used here as a bath soak, the seaweed tones and re-mineralizes the body.

0.9 oz (25 g) dried kombu
muslin bag

Infuse the kombu in a bowl of hot water for 10 minutes while you run a bath.

Pour the infused water into the bath through the muslin bag, catching the seaweed. Tie the top of the bag shut so you can put it into the bath to keep infusing as you soak.

INDEX